Information Security Primer for Managers

Information Security Primer for Managers

Ola Osunkoya, Ph.D

Information Security Primer for Managers

ISBN 978-0-6151-7019-0

@Copyright 2007

It is illegal to reproduce any part of this book without the written permission of the author

E-infoseckonsult publishing

109 Pine Cone court

Cedar brook, NJ 08081

Information Security Primer for Managers

Acknowledgement

This book is dedicated to my God who is the head of my life and has spared me through his grace to see this day even in my polluted blood, my loving wife, Olufunke Osunkoya, who never gave up on me when I was acting a fool, who always have a word of encouragement when I'm feeling weary, who goes to war with me despite all the odds that may be against us, my daughter, Tomisin Osunkoya, who has taught me patience and has given me a reason and a purpose for fatherhood and to my spiritual parents, Dr. Lamont Mclean and Pastor Connie Mclean who through their obedience to teach and live the Word of God, I have been able to raise up a Godly family by following their faith.

Information Security Primer for Managers

Foreword

You've heard the saying "Image is everything". It's a strong statement that means you must pay attention to the basic things like appearance. Everybody knows that the right outfit can make the difference, because appearance says a lot about a person. However, in the business world we have to learn to stop looking at the surface.

Any company will tell you that its brand, logo and image, is everything to their shareholders, the market and to their customers. It takes a long time to develop that reputation and brand loyalty. Mess it up and you'll go from Wall Street darling to a penny stock. This classic trust relationship is built on the ability to rely on the strength, truth and character of that organization.

To protect that trust and fundamentally, the image of the organization, security managers are often asked to abide by regulatory laws, sort through management discrepancies and technical issues, in an effort to safeguard the company's assets and reputation. Some are performing this feat without academic training, clear understanding of compliance issues and how the technical side of security is actually performed. These are the intended audience of *Information Security Primer for Managers*.

The author has provided this publication as a resource to prepare managers for the responsibility of an organization's security, filling in the void left from academic deficiency while providing insightful references. Utilization of this book should improve your overall experience when dealing with security related issues and brings with it the expertise of a professional well versed in many areas of the security field.

God bless you, and I am hopeful that this book will aid your career growth and maintain your organizations image.

Information Security Primer for Managers

Roger White, Msc CISA CISSP

Information Security Primer for Managers

Table of Content

Introduction- Information Security Introduction 7

Chapter 1- Information Security Overview 8

Chapter 2- Information Security Policy 10

Chapter 3- Hybrid Security Policy 12

Chapter 4- Cryptography 14

Chapter 5- Cryptographic key management 17

Chapter 6- Authentication 21

Chapter 7- Identity representation 24

Chapter 8- Access Control 26

Chapter 9- Security Confinement 28

Chapter 10- Evaluation models 30

Chapter 11- Security Assurance 33

Chapter 12- Malicious Logic 36

Chapter 13- Vulnerabilities 39

Chapter 14- Auditing 42

Chapter 15- Intrusion detection system 45

Chapter 16- Network Security 47

Chapter 17- Systems Security 49

Chapter 18- User Security 51

Chapter 19- Program Security 53

References 55

Information Security Primer for Managers

Introduction

Information Security –Why Managers should be Concerned

It is appropriate to begin the discussion by defining what information security is, why organizations need to protect their assets and what should be protected.

Thomas Peltier defined Information Security as a process of preventing assets from being disclosed to, modified by unauthorized parties and the recovery thereof, whether intentional or unintentional. Another definition states that it is a combination of concepts, techniques and technical measures employed in protecting assets from deliberate or unintentional acquisition, damage, disclosure or manipulation.

Organizations need to protect their assets because those assets are what it uses to achieve its business objectives. Management makes decisions based on information, the loss or unauthorized disclosure may reduce their competitive edge in the market. Corporations recognize the fact that disruptions to their business mean loss of revenue and probably loss of confidence by their customers; hence they implement a business continuity plan. Every business has legal and statutory responsibilities. One of such statutes is the foreign corrupt practices act which requires that all transactions affecting corporate information must be authorized by the management. An unauthorized transaction will put the onus on the organization to prove due diligence in their mode of operation.

Security of assets should be based on the level of impact the loss of that asset will have on the company. This is why a risk analysis is needed to categorize and label assets according to criticality. Protection must be based on the asset value, impact level and the likelihood of the loss happening.

Information Security Primer for Managers

Chapter 1

Information Security Overview

In this chapter, we introduce the three basic concepts of computer security, which are confidentiality, integrity and availability. The rest of the chapter expands on all the supporting and implementation principles of these concepts.

Confidentiality is described as hiding any information that you want to keep secret from the public eye. Confidentiality principle was prevalent in the government operation until the advent of e-commerce when companies started doing a lot of business on the Internet.

Implementation of the confidentiality principle is done using a mode of access control called cryptography. It uses the keys exchanged between two hosts to make a cipher version of the information to be exchanged. This process, apart from achieving confidentiality, authenticates the hosts involved at the time of key exchange by checking the time stamp.

The second principle is the integrity of the information being exchanged. In other words, how can I trust the information sent to me and how correct is that information? Mechanism to enforce this principle can either be a detection or prevention one or both. Prevention mechanism is achieved via the use of authentication and authorization, and it is mostly used for the purpose of trust aspect of integrity. Detection is not concerned with blocking unauthorized users trying to change that information. Instead, it focuses on the analysis of system events and verifying whether the data continue to be trustworthy or not.

Availability is the last principle, and it focuses on the existence of the information at the time needed by those who must have access to it. Failure to achieve this principle is called denial of service.

The author further presented attack concepts that will actually affect the achievement of

Information Security Primer for Managers

those three security principles. These are defined as threats or events which may take advantage of existing vulnerabilities. These threats range from snooping of information, to masquerading, repudiation of origin and denial of service.

Being able to combat these threats require two components- security policy and security mechanism. The policy describes a high level version of the rules of engagement while the mechanism is used to turn the policy wording into technical implementation that does the access control. However, companies, in an attempt to create security programs using these two components, will be faced with both operational and human challenges. Some of the operational challenges facing the security program are:

1. Doing a cost-benefit analysis. What do we stand to loose if the resource is lost as a result of insecurity? The cost of securing the resources must be less than what the company stand to loose as a result of insecurity.
2. Doing a risk analysis of the resources to be protected. What is the level of risk and the probability that the perceived event will occur?
3. Investigate the various laws and customs concerning the proposed security of that resource. A while back, there was a limit on cryptographic exports that uses more than 40 bit keys from the US to other countries.

The human challenges stems from the fact that security in itself, does not provide a direct financial reward for the company. The benefits are only seen when they are faced with losses resulting from insecurity. The company's employees also present some challenges because of changes required of them in the way they see those resources and the impact their carelessness may have on the company.

Information Security Primer for Managers

Chapter 2

Information Security Policy

Policy was first introduced in chapter one while discussing computer security overview. In this chapter, the focus will be on different types of policies, the role of trust as it relates to creating and understanding a policy and types of access control that a typical policy deals with.

A security policy is a statement that describes what a company will and will not allow in its environment. It divides the system into secure and insecure states by considering all aspects of confidentiality, integrity and availability.

Two types of security policies will be discussed; confidentiality and integrity or commercial policy. Organizations use one of these policies depending on their line of business and what is important in that environment. For example, the governments, including military's security policy tend to be biased towards confidentiality, probably because of the highly sensitive information that is being dealt with on a daily basis. Confidentiality policy's focus is privacy and does not deal with the trustworthiness of information that is hidden. This is addressed with the integrity or commercial security policy. The type of policy is prevalent in a commercial environment because of the desire to prevent tampering with their data. For example, this policy requires a database to always be in a consistent state throughout the flow of transaction. If the transaction did not complete, it is expected that data will revert back to what it used to be before the start of that transaction.

Any security policy is based on assumptions that users of the policy needs to be made aware for it to be effective. When these assumptions are not clearly understood, the users may make unintended conclusions about what is required by the policy. One of such policy assumption is trust. Microsoft comes up with patch for their operating system fairly often. An administrator assumes that the patch has been tested by the vendor and that it fixes the problem using it in a similar environment under the same circumstance. If any of these assumptions are not correct, it invalidates the requirement of the policy which the administrator is trying to comply with by keeping the system secure with patches and updates.

Organizations create security policies for the sole purpose of controlling access to their environment. There are two types of access control that may be used within the security policy either individually or in combination. They are mandatory access control and discretionary access control.

Discretionary access control can be described as originator based control. For example, if I create a directory, and I'm able to control access to the objects of the directory based on the identity of the subjects, this is a discretionary access control.

In the second type of access control, which is mandatory, identity does not play a key role. The operating system decides who can access and who will be denied access. As long as the administrator places subjects in the right security policy module and they are not allowed to change the security attributes, the operating system will effectively control access. Essentially, the control responsibility is removed from individuals and placed on the system.

Information Security Primer for Managers

Chapter 3

Hybrid Security Policy

Chapter 2 introduced two types of policy which addressed either confidentiality or integrity but not both. Most corporations have need for a policy that can address these two principles; hence the hybrid policy.

This chapter discusses four models of that hybrid policy while briefly comparing them with the bell-lapadula and the Clark-Wilson models. The models are Chinese wall, the clinical information security, the originator controlled access control and the role-based access control also known as RBAC.

Under the Chinese wall policy model, trying to avoid conflict of interest in business is the focus. Using a real estate example, if a realtor represents both the seller and the buyer, because he has pertinent information on both parties, the best interest of both clients will conflict and the realtor knowingly or unknowingly may use that information to help one client at the other's expense. The model dynamically establishes the access right of a user based on what he has already accessed. For example, if I worked for a bank that advised two competing oil companies (A & B), as an analyst, I can read the data of either company as long as the data set does not belong to a conflict of interest class and if they do, I will be allowed access to company A's data set only if I have not already accessed company B's data. This is the fundamental difference between this model and the Bell-Lapadula which has and keeps no record of past access.

Personal health information has the same confidentiality and integrity requirement just like an investment bank, but for different reasons and in a different way. Conflict of interest is not central in the implementation of a clinical information security policy, however privacy and correctness of the information is essential. The model deals with controlling access to patients' medical record. It requires a list of health workers who can read and those who can append to that record with a notification of the patient required anytime a change is made to the list.

Originator controlled access model was introduced because the industry felt there was a need for originators of data to be able to authorize the use of their data. If user A created document X and gives user B access, there was nothing stopping user B from giving user C access to the same data without the consent or approval of user A. Originators and not owners retain the control over the specific document. Documents may be owned as a result of acquisition from the originator, but dissemination requires approval from the originator. Mandatory and discretionary access control which focuses on centralized policy, did not address this situation. This is a decentralized type of policy since there will be several originators throughout the organization.

The final policy model is based on roles within an organization. Role based access control relies on giving access based on groups or job function instead of individual authorization. All security engineers in my organization have the same access, no matter where they work. This model focuses on the object being accessed rather than the subject as in the case of both the Chinese and clinical information models.

Chapter 4

Cryptography

In this discussion of cryptography, we will attempt to define the concept, support it with the history of cryptosystems from classical cryptography to the well known realm of public key cryptography and the cryptographic checksum.

The author described cryptography as the use of lock and key to secure a message from eavesdropping or from anyone who does not know the key. It is the process of keeping information secret and concealing its meaning. If information is significant enough to remain out of the public realm cryptography steps in to keep the information private. A good cryptographic system will defend against a cipher text only attack where the attacker knows only the cipher text, a known plain text attack where the attacker has both the cipher text and the plain text and a chosen plain text attack where the attacker enciphers a part of the plain text given the corresponding cipher text.

In it simplest form, cryptography is implemented using symmetric or single key. This means that both encryption and decryption will use the same key. Classical cryptosystems used this type of cryptography. A popular example that comes to mind is Caesar shift cipher. This was a very simple process of substituting one letter for another and the person that the information is being sent to will also know the key for the shift. For example, if Alice wants to send the word "hello" to Bob, she may decide to shift the letters by 3 (the key), the word now becomes "khoor". Of course, Bob will have to know the key to decrypt the message. Another classical cryptosystem is the transposition cipher which keeps the original letters but shifts their positions so that the end result is unreadable. Using the same key of 3, the word "Caesar shift" would become a cipher text of "sarshi ftcae". These encryption standards were weak and easily breakable; hence the introduction of a new symmetric encryption algorithm called data encryption standard (DES).

    DES was designed to encrypt sensitive but non-classified data. It is a block cipher based on the Feistel cipher. It uses the combination of substitution and transposition discussed earlier to implement four different modes, electronic codebook, cipher block chaining, cipher feedback and output feedback. DES uses 56 bit key length to offer 2^{56} possible keys or approximately $7.2 * 10^{16}$. It uses 16 rounds and each round has a new key also called a sub key which is based on the original key. A plain text is divided into two halves, the right half has one copy sent to the function algorithm, XORed with the left half. The end result of the XOR becomes the new right half. Once all the data has passed through the rounds, the two sides are swapped to produce the resultant cipher text.

    Symmetric algorithm does not scale well in a large environment without the use of some type of key distribution center which in turn introduces another complexity and a new point of failure. This is one of the several reasons that the public key infrastructure was introduced in 1976 by Diffie-Hellman. PKI relies on two keys, which is why it is called asymmetric cryptography. One key is used for encryption and a different key is used for decryption. For this system to be secure, it must be computationally infeasible for one to resolve the decryption key given knowledge of the algorithm and the encryption key. It should also be noted that RSA also has another version of this cryptography system.

    Up until now, all the discussion has been based on keeping the information secret which achieves confidentiality. However, if Alice receives a data from Bob because it says so, she cannot verify that the data that was sent by Bob is what she has. She only knows it was kept secret. Cryptographic checksum allows us to verify the integrity of the content. It protects

Information Security Primer for Managers

organizations against masquerade, content modification and sequence modification attacks. A fingerprint of the message is created by a hashing algorithm such as MD5 or SHA-1 and tampering with the message will produce a different message digest when Alice calculates it.

Information Security Primer for Managers

Chapter 5

Cryptographic Key Management

Cryptographic systems are as secure as the keys used in their algorithms. The keys need to be well managed for us to have confidence that there has not been a break in the chain of trust; hence the end result is secure. The discussion in this chapter focuses on private and public key exchange procedures, key storage, key revocation and using digital signatures with private and public key infrastructures.

As we have seen in classical cryptography, both parties to the conversation must have the same key. A method of exchanging this key must exist and it must remain hidden from unauthorized parties. Oftentimes, the keys need to be changed in order to maintain security in the event that a key is compromised. This process requires good key management. If Alice and Bob want to communicate using secret key or symmetric key cryptography system, they can both choose a key and bring it directly to each other. This does not scale well in a large environment. Classical cryptography relies on trusted third party that will choose keys and bring it directly to Bob and Alice. Most companies use a key distribution center (KDC) as the trusted third party. Figure 1 shows an illustration of KDC key generation process for Alice and Bob.

Information Security Primer for Managers

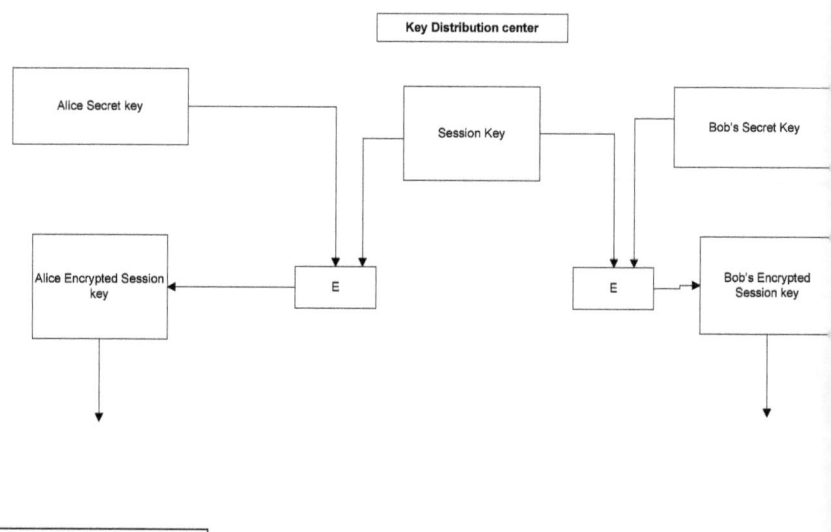

Figure 1- Session key generation by the KDC

Alice and Bob each have a shared unique secret key with the KDC. Alice lets the KDC know a secure message is to be sent to Bob. The KDC will generate a random session key and encrypt it twice. Once using Alice's secret key and once using Bob's secret key. Both copies are sent to Alice. She decrypts her version of the session key and sends Bob the session key that was encrypted with Bob's secret key. Finally, Alice encrypts her message with her decrypted session key and sends the message to Bob. On the other side, Bob has received two messages from Alice, his session key encrypted with his secret key and message from Alice. Bob decrypts his session key with his own secret key and uses that decrypted session key to decrypt the message sent by Alice.

Information Security Primer for Managers

The process described above does not scale well and the very presence of a KDC does weaken the overall cryptography system. This is another point of failure on the network. In the asymmetric cryptography world, key exchanges seem a lot cleaner and easier. All users have access to every other user's public key. All users have their own private key that is never revealed outside the local system. Alice generates a plain text on her computer and encrypts it with Bob's public key and sent to Bob. Upon receipt, Bob uses his private key to perform the decryption. The public key has to be in a secure repository managed by a trusted third party. Most companies that use asymmetric cryptography engage the service of a certificate authority. This authority verifies the identity of the public key owner by signing that public key.

Figure 2

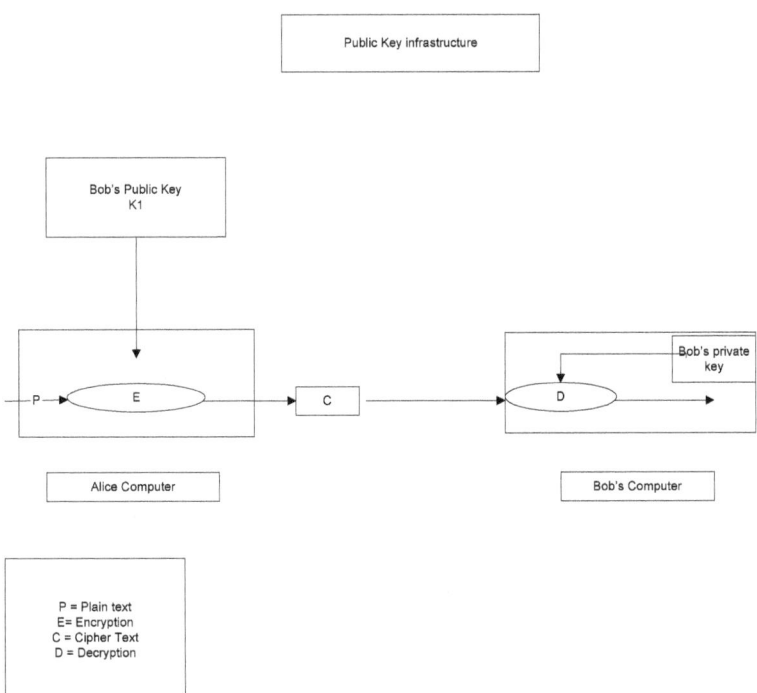

Information Security Primer for Managers

Knowing what we know about the importance of the various keys used in different cryptographic systems, it is imperative that we restrict access to them anywhere they are stored. Private keys are very important in the PKI scheme. These keys can either be stored in the system using operating system's control to limit access or it can be stored outside of the system using storage card like smart cards. The former method can be broken by defeating the ACL on the operating system which is done regularly these days. It is recommended that those key should be stored outside the system that uses them.

Since security can never be 100%, we need to prepare for those times that our keys may become compromised or when the keys are no longer valid due to expiration. This is the process of revocation. Revoking a key means that all communication encrypted using that key will be rejected. There has to be a well connected infrastructure of servers in place to notify all concerned parties when a key is revoked. All certificate authority maintains a certificate revocation list that is regularly updated although a time lag is experienced, but all in all, it prevents an invalid key from being used for too long before it is detected.

Up until this point all discussion has been centered on the confidentiality of information. If the communication between Alice and Bob is a legal contract, we will need a way to prove that those communication, although, confidential, indeed came from the parties involved. This is where digital signature comes in. This is the authentication of both origin and content. This is achieved by creating a message digest of the content using MD5 or SHA-1. This hash is then encrypted using the sender's private key. The recipient decrypts the encrypted hash using the sender's public key. He then recalculates the hash and if there's a difference, the information is not exactly what was sent from the known sender.

Information Security Primer for Managers

Chapter 6

Authentication

In any network, one underlying technology that has to be addressed is that of authentication. In this chapter, I describe three types of those authentication method, password, challenge-response and biometrics.

Authentication can be described as a process or system by which users can prove and verify specific information, such as who they are. For example, when doing business transaction with a credit card on the phone, you may be asked for the billing address of the card to gain access to your account. Although this is not a strong form of authentication, it does provide authentication. In authentication, an external entity is making a claim of specific identity to be bound to a subject. The system that performs the authentication takes the user's claim and matches that to a database of records. This is a one-to-one mapping. Depending on your environment, authentication may be done using what you know, what you have, what you are or a combination of these three things.

Passwords are the most popular type of "what you know". Every user of networks and the Internet is aware of passwords. Since authentication is supposed to identify the designated subject, passwords should be kept secret. This is an example of a shared secret within a network since the secret is only known to the user and the authenticating server. The network user remembers the secret and enters it when requested. The server compares this secret with the one it knows for the user and if there is a match, the user is allowed into the system.

Although password-based authentication is very simple, it is also a very weak form of authentication because of its susceptibility to compromise. Eavesdropping or sniffing password is a common attack which is always a prelude for a more devastating attack of the network.

Information Security Primer for Managers

Password normally has long lifespan which gives an attacker enough time to guess or brute force the correct one. Companies that are building trusted network recognize this weakness and are opting to use a combination of what you have and what you know (two-factor authentication), a password that is only valid once (one-time password) or what you are (Biometrics).

A one time password, as the name implies, is only valid for one use, so if it is captured by sniffing, it is no longer useful in the hand of the attacker. The only issue in using this is that it has administration overhead because several passwords need to be generated and also synchronized with the authenticating server.

A more secure way of doing authentication with less overhead is to use a two factor authentication which can be time-based or challenge-response based. In a challenge-response system, an authenticating server sends a random challenge to the user who computes a response using hardware or software token, the user then sends the response back to the server. The server, using the same algorithm as the token, computes the random challenge and if it gets the same response as the one sent from the client, the user is allowed into the system. The second type of two-factor authentication uses a time based procedure. The user takes a code generated by the token, adds a pin number which creates a pass code combined with a seed value and the current time encrypted and sent to the server. The server authenticates the user by generating its own version of valid of valid code by accessing the pre-registered PIN and using the same seed value and algorithm to validate the user.

Biometrics can be used for authentication or identification. This is using physical characteristics to authenticate or identify a user. We are only concerned with the authentication use for the purpose of this chapter. Using biometrics require the enrollment of the user, creating a template from the raw data collected and matching the template with whatever is presented at the time of authentication. Depending on various factors, one can use fingerprints, voices, eyes (Iris and retinal), faces, keystrokes (pattern of hitting keys) or a combination of any of the above-mentioned. Biometrics however, has its downside and this explains why it is not widely used in the corporate world. Failure to enroll, false match, false non-match and the time it takes to authenticate are some of those issues. These problems re-introduce security risks like denial of service that companies are looking to avoid by employing strong authentication mechanisms like biometrics.

Information Security Primer for Managers

Chapter 7

Identity Representation

Having discussed authentication, we need to delve a little deeper on what is used to achieve that authentication. This chapter focuses on those objects/subjects in computer science which are used to represent identity in the process of authentication and authorization such as files and objects, users, groups and roles, certificates used for public key infrastructure and web identities.

For authentication to be valid, the subject being represented by the identity has to be unique. This is done by binding a principal to an identity representation. An identity, correctly represented, is able to provide uniqueness to a given subject/object because the system must search through a given database or record in order to find a match. This is called a many-to-one mapping. Identities are used for the purpose of different representations, two of which are accountability, for logging and auditing and access control for authentication and authorization.

To do proper logging, auditing, authentication and authorization, files and objects must be identified. Operating systems differ in the ways they identify objects. UNIX identifies all it objects as files and directories, while Microsoft differentiates between files, directories and drivers. UNIX represents a user in terms of a number called UID while Microsoft is not so stringent on what it uses to represent a user ID, anything will be accepted save some special characters which are excluded.

Another way that identities are represented is using a collection of entities as one, otherwise referred to as groups and roles. Sometimes, we need to share files or coordinate some projects with other people we work with. This can be done by creating groups or roles that is represented by an identity and authorizing only that principal to access the project's object.

Digital certificates are also used to represent users with cryptographic keys. A certificate is like a driver's license which has all information that binds the license to you. A trusted third party creates, distributes and revokes digital certificate (Certificate authority) just like a licensing authority. The certificates are issued to users who can prove their identity and credentials.

Finally, the web is one place that has diverse ways of representing identities. The Internet requires the host to be identified, users need identity, and even the data being passed by the host is sometimes bound to a principal. Web host identification is synonymous with domain name service (DNS), which translates friendly names to Internet packet address and vice versa. Internet merchants are always looking for ways to enhance user experience. Such web sites monitor your surfing habits and create cookies of those places you visited. Cookies also maintain states, so that it remembers where you were during a transaction even if you got out of that web site and returned at a later time.

Information Security Primer for Managers

Chapter 8

Access Control

In order for an authentication procedure to be effective, there has to be a control of access to the system. This chapter examines the mechanisms used to do access control by discussing the creation of access control list, the capabilities and different types of access control.

Access control provides security authentication and authorization for objects against processes trying to read, write or execute them. Access control can either be physical or logical. Our discussion focuses on the logical aspect of the controls.

Access control mechanisms usually utilize authorization table also referred to as access control lists. This refers to a register of users (including groups, machines, and processes) who have permission to use a particular system resource and the type of access permitted. The following table illustrates a typical access control list.

Figure1: Access control list table

	Users A	**User B**	**User C**
File A	Read, execute	Read	write
File B	Read, execute	Execute	Read
File C	Read, execute	Read, wrrite, execute	Read

Every user in the table is associated with a list. User A can read and execute all files in the system, while users B and C are limited except for file C where user B has full control. Depending on the policy of the organization, these lists are constructed on the principles of least privileges. Unfortunately, not all systems can implement a granular control to support the security policy. These systems end up with abbreviated controls which give more privileges to some processes than what is needed to perform the job.

Access control lists vary considerably in their capabilities and flexibility. Some only allow specifications for certain preset groups (e.g. owner, group and world); while more advanced ones allow much more flexibility, such as user-defined groups which are more granular even to the level of individuals. This type of access controls are discretionary in nature (implemented by the security administrator or individual owners of the object).

Most systems that were developed with security in mind have some type of access list implementation built in. The three access list implementation discussed in this chapter are lock and key, ring based and propagated access control.

Lock and key access control is prevalent on Cisco routers. It is a traffic filtering security feature that is used to dynamically filter IP traffic. Particular information is associated with the resource (the lock) and the subject that needs to access the resource must have information (the key) to unlock access. When the subject tries to access the object, the key presented is checked to see if it corresponds to the object lock and the appropriate level of access is granted.

Propagated access control is mostly used in an environment that has a policy of originator controlled access. A document created by user A has PACL attached to the document and only user A can change the attributes of the PACL. Any other user that reads the document is tracked by addition of another PACL attribute forming a chain that can be linked back to the owner.

Information Security Primer for Managers

Chapter 9

Security Confinement

The principle of least privilege deals with confinement of access to only the allowed processes. Access control helps enforce this principle based on a well defined policy of authentication and authorization. I explore the issue of security confinement and suggested ways to counter the problem by using virtual machines, sandboxes and other detection controls of covert channels.

Security confinement problem is described as the device inability to prevent data from being leaked to unauthorized process (including groups and users). A client should be able to request information from a server without the server leaking the information to unauthorized process in the course of fulfilling the request. Solving the confinement issue requires that we know every entry into and exit out of an application. This includes any unintended communication or storage path also referred to as a covert channel. Maintaining a security confinement becomes harder when we take into consideration the fact that it has to be transitive (user A invokes a confined process A, if process A has to invoke process B, the new process should also remained confined as the original process). As stated above, this problem can be resolved to a very large extent, by isolation mechanisms and analysis of covert channels.

One isolation mechanism is the virtual machine which simulates the hardware of a computer system. A typical implementation is the VM ware which performs different processes within a confined process. The physical hardware only sees one process and monitors that process, so any process being executed within the virtual environment is separated from the normal hardware process. This implementation achieves a transitive security confinement.

The second type of isolation mechanism is the sandbox and operates for all intent and purposes, like the VM ware. A java virtual machine is a good example of how a sandbox works. Applets are downloaded into this sandbox and are allowed to be executed based on the JVM security policy and the configuration of the applet itself.

Covert channel presents a different challenge because it has to be detected before it can be blocked or monitored. This is sometimes difficult when we realize that we are dealing with communication and/or storage path that are not intended to be used as such. The use of a packet flow mechanism with detail analysis can help detect a covert channel. If the covert channel cannot be eliminated, it is suggested that it should be made less useful by reducing the capacity or the ability of a hacker to make any sense of what is being processed.

Information Security Primer for Managers

Chapter 10

Evaluation Models

Security is a function of assurance and assurance relies on the corporate security policy which is brought to life by the security mechanism implementation. Security mechanism does not equal a secure environment, there has to be a measurement of what is secure and what is not in an environment. Defining and describing that measurement is the focus of this chapter. I will attempt to describe assurance as it relates to trust in a network and explored ways of building a trusted network using some of the popular models in the industry.

We can only be assured of a trustworthy network if we have enough evidence to support such. We get this evidence by creating or using standards by which our environment will be measured against such as system security engineering capability maturity model, the trusted computer system evaluation criteria and the information technology security evaluation criteria. Assurance is needed because of the inherent flaws in our systems, unintentional configuration that violates the policy by administrators and intentional compromise of those security mechanisms.

The industry standards used in the assurance evaluation tries to show that the system implemented and the one in operation remains one and the same throughout the life of that system. The standards focus on four main aspects of development life cycles; policy assurance, which ensures that the requirements are complete and consistent. Design assurance will ensure that design is sufficient to translate what is in the policy into implementation. Implementation assurance gives the evidence of meeting the policy requirement and also consistent with the design. Operational assurance is the evidence that daily administration does not move the system from the secure state of the known policy to an insecure state.

Information Security Primer for Managers

The most popular and one of the oldest assurance approaches is the waterfall life cycle model widely used for developing business applications. It is based on a systematic, sequential approach to systems development that begins with feasibility studies and progresses through requirement definition, system and software design, implementation and unit testing, integration and system testing, operation and maintenance. The series of steps or phases have defined goals and activities to perform with assigned responsibilities. However, problems were encountered using this approach and led to the development of other models. Some of the problems are:

1. unanticipated events, since real projects rarely follow the sequential flow prescribed
2. Inability to get the proper requirements as the approach requires.
3. Customers are often impatient since the system is not available until late in the project life cycle.

Given the above-mentioned issues, new models were created to address them. The models are:

- ◊ Prototyping – It is used to build a working model that elicit/verify requirements and explore design issues. Eventually, the prototype is hardened so that it can be implemented in production or recoded based on learning from the prototype.
- ◊ Extreme programming – This involves building the system in iterations or increments with feedback occurring after each increment. This model is driven by business decisions.
- ◊ System assembly and reusable components – This models relies on existing components to do the build. The rationale behind this is that it is better to build a trusted solution from existing trusted components. This is more like putting together a piece of puzzle than creation. It requires greater analysis of existing component security and how it can be integrated into the new policy requirement.

◊ Exploratory programming – It uses a series of prototype to develop a solution to the point of detailed design, build and test. The solution spirals out from the initial limited prototype to become progressively more expansive and detailed.

Information Security Primer for Managers

Chapter 11

Security Assurance

Assurance of security is the goal of any security program. We all want an impeccable security of our intellectual information, but that is not possible. What is achievable, however, is to know that the organization is following some type of industry standard in its quest to be safe from hackers. Formal evaluation of any system against well known evaluation models such as trusted computer system evaluation criteria (TCSEC), the common criteria (CC), systems security engineering capability maturity model (SSE-CMM) and FIPS, help us arrive at a trusted level of security assurance.

The trusted computer system evaluation criteria were the first major evaluation system used by the United States government. Although, the criteria were based on evaluating government systems, it did contribute and help define commercial product evaluation. It has two main requirements: functional, which includes, discretionary access control, mandatory access control, object reuse, identification and authentication, trusted path and audit requirement. The second is the assurance requirement of configuration management, trusted distribution, design specification and verification, testing and product documentation. Systems may be evaluated for seven different classes: A1, B1, B2, B3, C1, C2, and D. The evaluation process was divided into three stages (application, preliminary technical review and evaluation), and the evaluation stage was further divided into sub stages: design analysis, test analysis and final review. TCSEC had scope and process limitations which led to the creation of other evaluation standards. The biggest limitation was the fact that it only addressed confidentiality while the issue of integrity was not touched. The process also took too long to complete.

Information Security Primer for Managers

Due to some of the issues mentioned above, TCSEC was retired by the government and the common criteria (CC) became the United States evaluation standard in 1998. The purpose of the criteria is to allow organizations to demonstrate that their product conforms to the stated security target. The model supports two types of evaluation methodologies:

1. Evaluation of protection profiles, which permits the implementation of security requirements for a set of products that, must fully comply with a set of specific security objectives. The protection profile could be developed by the user community, IT developers or any interested party. The only requirement is that the product has to have an evaluation assurance level (EAL), which defines the rigors that must be applied to the product development before presenting it for evaluation. The EAL has seven levels of assurance from being functionally tested to formally verified design and tested.

2. Evaluation of security target. This is a requirement to document the security functionality of the product and the environment in which the product will operate. Security target is mostly developed from the protection profile, but it can also be developed by referencing the common criteria functional or assurance components.

Despite the completeness of the common criteria model, it suffered from criteria creep. This is supposedly managed by the project board; unfortunately, the effectiveness depends on the motivation of every team members of that board.

Common criteria only defined the requirements for security functionality. The security industry was looking to advance security engineering and needed a model that will define requirements for security evaluation process. The systems engineering capability maturity model did just that and it became an ISO standard in 2002. This model gave security engineers a way to support assurance and confidence to trust the system. The model is based on eleven processes of evaluation and five capability maturity levels ranging from ad hoc, where success depends solely on individual efforts to optimizing, where the organization has attained the ability to quantitatively control its security process.

All the measurement models mentioned above did not address the evaluation of cryptographic modules which was needed since they are part of the security mechanisms being measured. The federal information processing standard 140-2 (FIPS 140-2) was created for this purpose. The standard defines the requirements that must be met by any cryptographic module used to protect unclassified information. There are four levels of security defined within the requirement. The first level, which is the lowest level, only requires that encryption algorithm be FIPS approved. The second level requires a tamper evident physical security and an authentication of the operator based on role. Level three went further on authentication by requiring that access to the physical area should be based on individual authentication and level four includes all the requirement of the previous levels plus an envelope of protection around the cryptographic module. It also requires organization to protect against fluctuations in the production environment.

Information Security Primer for Managers

Chapter 12

Malicious Logic

We have been discussing the process of securing our environment by using security policy, various types of security mechanism and even evaluating our systems to get an assurance of how secure those systems we introduce into our environments. This chapter explores some of the reasons why we go through these troubles by discussing the threat of malicious logic which include but not limited to Trojan horse, computer virus and computer worms with the countermeasures that we can employ to mitigate these attacks.

Matt bishop (2004) described malicious logic as an instruction that will make a secure environment transition into an insecure state as a result of its execution. This is what a Trojan horse does. It is an unauthorized program contained within a legitimate program. The unauthorized program performs functions unknown (and probably unwanted) by the user. Trojan horse will do anything that the user who executes it has including, deleting files, transmitting files to a remote location and installing programs on the network that gives covert access. Trojan horse works similar to client-server model. It comes in two parts, a client and a server part. The attacker deploys the client to connect to the server which runs on the remote machine when the remote user unknowingly executes the program on the machine. Trojan horse typically uses the TCP/IP protocol, but UDP is sometimes employed as well.

While a Trojan horse requires the help of a program to propagate itself, another version of the program inserts itself into files without the help of any program. This is called a computer virus. It inserts a malicious program code into other executable code that can self-replicate and spread from computer to computer via sharing of storage media, transfer of logic over telecommunication lines or direct contact with an infected machine/code. Another variation of Computer virus installs itself into memory and hooks file access calls which infect executable files that are opened at the time. The virus triggers routine that overwrites data on all installed hard drives. It uses direct disk writes calls to achieve this and bypasses standard BIOS virus protection while overwriting the MBR and boot sector.

Another well-known variation of malicious logic is the computer worm which is more destructive than virus. It destroys data and utilizes tremendous computer and communication resources, but do not replicate like virus. Worms do not change other programs, but can run independently and travel from machine to machine across network connection. They may be centralized or distributed in nature.

New models are always being proposed in the security industry to counter these malicious codes since the hackers are constantly refining their attacks. Some of the suggestions in the book are technical, but one cannot ignore the benefit of educating the users and spending some time on fine tuning the business process. Having said that, the following technical countermeasures help to mitigate the vulnerabilities:

1. Malicious logics are effective only when they are executed; limiting the objects that can be accessed by a user will go a long way in stifling the damage that may be caused by malicious code execution.
2. Limiting the distance that a data may flow via a flow distance metric. This causes a slow of propagation to any malicious code.
3. Through education, users should learn to reduce their rights when running suspect programs. Without excessive rights, malicious logics cannot go far into the kernel to affect the system.

Information Security Primer for Managers

4. Apply a code to files that will get a signature on those files when they are first installed. The code will also run at set intervals and any change to the files will be flagged as possible attack. Tripwire is one of the products that do this. Most Linux operating systems have scaled down versions of the product.
5. Restrict the process of that object to a sandbox or reducing the priority of execution. This suggests that we have a security monitor on the system which will be able to determine that there is a policy violation.
6. Signature based programs that checks for known malicious logic also mitigate the risk. This is the most popular and the least effective because it does not catch unknown logic. Most commercial anti-virus products are in this class.

Information Security Primer for Managers

Chapter 13

Vulnerabilities

Malicious logics are threats that exist because of vulnerabilities associated with the use of information resources. Failure or lack of controls in a system results in vulnerability of that system. Vulnerabilities are characteristics of information resources that can be exploited by a threat to cause harm. The chapter focuses on ways of detecting vulnerabilities in a system by using formal verification and penetration testing with various frameworks for classifying vulnerabilities.

Formal verification is using the industry evaluation standards such as TCSEC, common criteria and FIPS to measure the assurance of security. It can also be likened to a process of creating a hypothesis, where you come up with a statement and prove the statement is right or wrong. In analyzing vulnerability in a system, the tester has to present a state at which the vulnerability will manifest once the test takes place. The condition is to have a program in a known secure state that will transition to an insecure state. Formal verification proves the absence of a flaw based on the security policy, it does not state that the system as a whole is free from vulnerabilities that the security policy is not concerned about.

Penetration testing is the second option of finding out whether your network or system is vulnerable to attacks or not. The goal is to use a combination of procedures and techniques typically used by hackers to violate or bypass the security of that network or system. There are three types of studies that can be conducted with penetration testing: we can study an attack that takes place from the external side of the network when the attacker has no knowledge or information of the network, an external attack against the system by someone who has access to that system and an internal attack from an authorized user. Typical components of a penetration

Information Security Primer for Managers

test may include open source intelligence gathering through publicly available discovery techniques to gain information on an organization's network, attempting to guess passwords using password cracking tools, searching for backdoors into host-based systems and exploiting known operating system vulnerabilities in network components and various type of servers that are web, application and database systems. The company's management should be informed of the use of this technique so that proper permission is obtained.

Correcting the flaws found using the formal verification and penetration testing should be done in the context of the test performed. A comprehensive review of the results and the security policy should be done so that proper correlation will lead to the correct remedy. Our ability to do this depends on how much we understand those vulnerabilities and their mode of operation. Various studies have come up with a number of frameworks that classifies the vulnerability mode of operation which makes it easier to recognize them and engage the appropriate policy and mechanism for remedy.

The RISOS study believes that vulnerabilities exploit a number of flaws in system development and administration such as incomplete parameter validation, inconsistent validation, sharing of privileged data, inadequate identification or authentication and logic errors. The second model called the protection analysis model classified the flaws into four categories of improper protection domain initialization, improper validation, improper synchronization and choice of operand used when operating the system. The NRL taxonomy categorized these flaws based on how they allow the vulnerability, when it actually manifests itself and where it is resident in the system. The final one called the Aslam model classified flaws into two categories of coding faults and emergent faults. The coding flaws are those introduced at the development stage such as validation and synchronization errors, while the emergent faults are those introduced during the systems administration into the configuration and the environment in which the system operates.

Information Security Primer for Managers

Chapter 14

Auditing

Ideally, we would like to discover attacks on our networks in real time, but sometimes this is not possible either because our security control in that area is not as strong or it was not an area that real time detection was needed. Auditing helps discover any attack or attempts that have been made against our systems by analyzing logs. The chapter explores the anatomy of a typical auditing system, principles of designing one and some examples of audit mechanisms.

Auditing in general, is best described as the function of measuring something against a standard. Our focus is using auditing to measure the security of a system against the policy of that system. In other words, auditing is asking yourself, "How do you know".

In order to build an audit system, three components are considered essential. A logger, which is really a snapshot of the system at any point in time, an analyzer can be a person or a tool and a notifying system. A good example of an audit tool is the intrusion detection system which logs all packet traffic in and out of the network including the payload. This tool is always used during incident response to quickly discover and put a stop to attacks.

When designing an audit system, the goal of the audit determines what the system will record. One thing that should be avoided in building an audit system is information overload. This can also make it difficult to discover what is important within the logged data. The second consideration is the baseline of the system to be audited. The system should be in a known good state before the snapshot is taken or else, all measurements will be against a corrupted system. The context of what is being logged should also be understood so that proper audit conclusions can be reached, for example, there are information that are time sensitive and once the time has passed, that information is no longer considered secret. If the information becomes public knowledge after the protected time, it is no longer a risk to the company. Finally, audit systems usually sanitize data sent to the notifying system. The sanitizer should be designed in a way that it does not strip out important data that should allow proper event correlation while protecting the confidential and private information of the organization. This is always a big issue when the organization log has to be given to an outside auditor.

Designing audits around systems that were built with security in mind is straightforward, however, most of the security issues we face today are the result of systems that were built without any security consideration (TCP/IP is one of them). Auditing these systems is based on two different goals. The first goal is to focus on violation of the organization security policy by checking for states that is contrary to the policy. This requires constant snapshot of the system being taken and compared to a known good state. If that model is not used, a transition check should be done. Every process execution has to be monitored to ensure that the system is returned to the known good static state. The second goal will focus on detection of known violations which is not in the policy. Working knowledge of these violations is required by the auditor. Fortunately, there are auditing tools that have been automated to make the task easier.

Most systems that are manufactured recently come with some type of audit mechanism, such as logs and even analyzers. For example, SunOS has been shipping with the basic security module since coming out with version 2.7. Cisco IOS has logging function that allows you to do cursory troubleshooting and audit. Microsoft OS has logging for application, system and security events which is very useful for systems administrators and also a good beginning for any auditor. These audit mechanisms are good but they rarely provide the level of details that is necessary to decipher some of the new vulnerabilities and attacks. Organizations tend to look outside for audit tools that compliments those provided by the system vendors.

Information Security Primer for Managers

Chapter 15

Intrusion Detection System

One of the tools that auditors consider invaluable because of the log details is the intrusion detection system. This chapter discussed the principles of intrusion detection, the three models used to build an intrusion mechanism, the architecture and organization of the system within the network.

As the organization builds complex interconnected networks where partners from the outside require access to the inside, where you have employees telecommunicating, and where you have internal connections to external suppliers, the problem grows. In order for networks to continue to grow and be functional, there must be a certain degree of trust built into the systems. However, on top of the level of trust, there must be verification of this trust. The method most often employed by organization these days is a solid intrusion detection system.

Intrusion is the unauthorized access to or activity in an information system. It can also be described as the improper use of resources inside the organization whether intentional or not. The process of detecting improper or unauthorized use of those resources is called intrusion detection.

There are three models used to analyze an intrusion: the anomaly model, which analyzes the characteristics of a particular behavior and compares them with expected values based on a standard or known patterns of use. The second model is uses known patterns of misuse to match a behavior. This type of intrusion detection system is the most popular, yet it is the least effective because it relies on prior knowledge of the type of attack (signature-based). The last model is based on analyzing misuse or unauthorized access based on the organization security policy. The analysis depends heavily on the ability to correlate analyzed packets to a security policy.

Information Security Primer for Managers

The architecture of an Intrusion detection system in a network of today consist of a group of processes working together and in virtually every case, these processes are on different computers and devices across the network. There are three basic components of an intrusion detection system: the sensor or agent which is often configured in promiscuous mode. The agent collects the packets from the network. The command console or director is where the system is monitored and managed. It maintains control over the intrusion detection components and it should be accessible from any location. The third component is the alert notifying system responsible for contacting the incident handler. Modern systems have the ability to provide alerts via pop-up windows, audible tones, paging, email, and simple network management protocol.

Placement of intrusion detection system in any organization depends on the security policy. An organization may feel that what is important to monitor reside on the hosts, therefore, the host-based approach is best for them, while another organization, based on their policy, may implement a combination of host-based and network intrusion detection. Another variation of implementation is the distributed model where the agents are located on the hosts and perform the analysis and report to the director. The downside is that the hosts may experience a bit of performance drop as the computer is engaged in this work constantly.

With the placement of the intrusion detection system, organizations need to devise a plan of response. Intrusion response goal is to minimize damage to company's asset and stop the attack. In general, there are three components of intrusion response in any organization. The first is to detect that there is an actual attack. Once the attack has been identified, the next step is to control the attack by confinement. With the attack now limited, it is time to respond by eradicating the attack and recover the system.

Information Security Primer for Managers

Chapter 16

Network Security

Having discussed all the principles necessary to create a computer security program in the previous chapters, I created a practical application of those principles from policy development, network security architecture based on the policy developed, type of networks attacks that may be experienced and how to anticipate and prepare for such attacks.

In developing a policy, all internal and external organizations that will be affected should be taken into consideration. The policy should be clear regarding the flow of information between those organizations and address the security issues that may occur. The object of protection, which is the data, must be properly classified based on the company's need and the subject (user) classes. Availability of the network and how it is addressed within the policy depends on what type of business the company does. Due to its multinational status, the sample company requires the network to be up 99% of the time, which means that the company's network will need the have redundancy built into it.

The network design of the sample organization was created to satisfy and reflect the policy requirements. Because the company does business on the Internet, and requires the public to access information on its web server, a demilitarized zone had to be created sandwiched between two firewalls, one protecting the company from the public and the other protecting the internal network from the demilitarized zone (DMZ). All servers that will be accessed by the public are placed within the DMZ. Within the internal network, five sub networks were created based on the data and user classifications since the principle of least privilege was being followed. Customer data can only be seen by those who are directly involved with the customers. Corporate data is only available to senior management. Both customer data and corporate data

Information Security Primer for Managers

may be made available to the developers when needed, but after proper approval by senior management. Access to the development subnet is through a trusted host that requires authentication and uses a secure shell protocol to encrypt data being transferred. This separates the production network from the development network.

As stated earlier, the availability of the network is just as important as the confidentiality and integrity of the protected data. Denial of service is one of the well known attacks that may disrupt the company's business. The mode of perpetrating this attack is to flood either the transport media or the application itself with requests that never completes (SYN flooding). The company should put mechanism in place to respond to this attack. Using the Linux operating system, a SYN cookie turned on will reduce the effect of this attack, while in the Cisco IOS, a configuration of TCP intercept with proper threshold set will do the same thing. The company also prepared for unanticipated attacks by placing log servers within the infrastructure and reviewing them often.

Information Security Primer for Managers

Chapter 17

Systems Security

It is not enough to secure the perimeter of any network and be assured of systems security. In our sample company, the policy requires that every piece of equipment that the data traverses must be secure, in other words, the implementation of the policy reflects defense-in-dept security principle.

Once the network security mechanism is in place, the company turned her attention to the systems used within the network. The chapter examines the policy created for two specific environments within the organization, the web server inside the DMZ and the development systems in the developer subnet and how to implement secure communication, users, files and process interactions between those systems.

According to the policy, the web server should run only web application process that allows the company customers to access information needed to do business, while trusted users (employees) who are authenticated using secure shell can administer the server. On the development systems, which are mainly UNIX-like operating systems, only authorized users may work on those systems. As noted in the previous chapter, the developers have a subnet for all their systems.

In other to implement this policy, most systems come with some type of access control list. This is what the company used to lock down access to the web server and the development systems. The company used apache web application, so they were able to leverage the access list in the web configuration file to deny access from the inside and allow access from the outside to HTTP request. Secure shell server daemon was turned on to accept authorized request for administration. On the development system, the TCP wrapper was used to specify hosts that can

49

Information Security Primer for Managers

connect to those systems.

User privilege was limited on both systems. The web server limited user access from the internet to only read the web pages. Logging was turned on for audit and accountability purpose. On the development system, each user has a unique identification (UID) which is being administered via a central repository called the network information server (NIS). This reduces the risk of having two users with the same UID on different systems, thereby making audit logs inaccurate.

Authentication for the purpose of administration of the web server is only accepted from a trusted UNIX host using the PAM module. Password aging was not implemented because the company thought it unnecessary. On the development systems, security is not so relaxed. Password aging and audit for easily guessed passwords is in place. One commonality between the two systems is the fact that strong authentication is used (SSH).

Processes running on the web server are limited to those required to serve web pages with the appropriate level of privileges and the SSH server daemon to accept secure shell request for administration. In contrast to the web server, the development systems run more processes because of their development function. However, those processes are owned by the "nobody" user which will not spawn a shell and has no home directory.

File security on the web server is handled by placing all the system files on a compact disc, so that any attack against the server will not alter the system. The developer systems all have standard builds which can be run from a bootable compact disc. This also prevents developers from altering the system. This approach relies on the physical security of the storage media.

Information Security Primer for Managers

Chapter 18

User Security

This chapter continued the process of building a trusted network. Having implemented a perimeter and a system security for our sample company, I will continue the trusted network build by focusing on user security, building access, file and device, process and electronic communication security mechanism with the user policy.

All access to the network or system should be identified and protected with some type of authentication. Users should be educated not to choose easily guessed passwords or write passwords down depending on where the systems are located. Generally, it is assumed that systems are in the open and therefore writing passwords and leaving them around the system is not considered a safe practice.

The security policy should also address the procedure for login to the systems. Attacks may be perpetrated easily if there is no mutual authentication, or the passwords may be visible to naked eyes and this is susceptible to shoulder surfing. Systems that display the last login time will also help users verify if their credential has been compromised.

User security process should also include awareness program. Users may not leave their systems unattended. In order for this to be effective, most systems have lock programs that will lock the screen after a set time of inactivity. Password is required to get back on the system once the program is enabled.

The system's file and directory permission settings should be used to control access by users. UNIX operating system is effective in doing this either based on users or group. The appropriate use of one or the other depends on how granular the policy requires access to be implemented. All storage devices within the system or that may have access to the system should have write access through them limited.

The processes manipulate objects and users should understand what the process is doing anytime they run it. For example, copying a file from a source to a destination creates a duplicate file including the permission, but when the same file is moved to another destination, the source no longer exist and the new file does not retain the permission. Some processes require authentication to start, all passwords in this case, should never be stored on the local machine in clear-text and the start up file access need to be limited to the owner of the process.

Operating systems are equipped with mail protocols that enable them to communicate electronically. Since electronic mails are generally considered untrustworthy, mail programs should never be allowed to automatically execute anything.

Information Security Primer for Managers

Chapter 19

Program Security

Process security was mentioned in the previous chapter as it relates to the users. However, users may observe all security guidelines in accessing a process, if the program that launches that process is insecure, the company has not done due diligence in securing the organization. Building a trusted network, like our sample company is trying to do is end to end. Program development or choosing the right program is a vital aspect of this process. This chapter explores the policy requirements, design, refinement and implementation, common security related programming problems, testing, maintenance and operation of the programs.

The policy requirement for any program that will be used on this network states that access must be based on user, location and time of request. This is to prevent unauthorized access with a compromised user account. The program must also be able to provide both restricted and unrestricted access so that authorized users within the restricted role cannot perform unrestricted actions on the system. The program should be able to prevent unauthorized changes by authorized users which prevent threats like Trojan horse execution.

A program design for this environment needs to be done in modules. Each of the policy requirements will be addressed individually. For example, we need to develop a program that will identify the user, use IP address or DNS name to put that user into a location and add a time stamp to the access request. This will be one of the modules of the program. Every module will deal with one requirement that will be put together once all the requirements are satisfied. The program development starts with a pseudo code that will be refined before it is coded in any programming language.

Information Security Primer for Managers

Programmers make mistakes or overlook some things while designing or coding programs. This is why we have so many vulnerabilities that are exploited on the network. To avoid the trend on this network, the framework for identifying and classifying vulnerabilities will be used. The protection analysis model was chosen for this company because of the technical nature of the analysis. The model examines improper choice of initial protection domain, improper isolation of implementation details, improper change which causes program to transition into insecure state, improper naming, when two objects have the same name, improper deletion, improper validation, improper sequencing and improper choice of operand and operation.

Once the program has been fully coded, testing must be done within the environment that the program will be used. Obviously, the program should not be tested in production, but the test environment needs to mimic that of production for proper result interpretation.

Assuming that we have an acceptable program, the code will be frozen so that what is distributed is what was certified. The frozen code has to be stored in an environment with logical and physical security.

Information Security Primer for Managers

References

Andrew Lockhart. (2004). *Network Security Hacks.* California: O'Reiley.

Bishop, M. (2004). *Introduction to Computer Security.* Boston, MA: Addison-Wesley.

Dmitry Bokotey, Andrew G. Mason, & Raymond Morrow. (2003). *CCIE Practical studies:Security.* Indianapolis, IN: Cisco Press.

Information systems audit and control association. (2005). *Cybercrime:Incident response and digital forensics.*

Keith J. Jones, Mike Shema, & Bradley C. Johnson. (2002). *Anti-hacker Toolkit.* Berkley, CA: McGraw-Hill.

Michael Cross, N. L. J., Tony Piltzecker. (2002). *Security+.* Rockland, MA: Syngress Publishing Inc.

Michael G. Solomon, Diane Barrett, & Neil Broom. (2005). *Computer Forensics Jumpstart.* New York: Sybex.

Warren G. Kruse, & Jay G. Heiser. (2002). *Computer Forensics: Incidence response essentials.* Boston: Addison-Wesley.

Warren Peterson. (2005). *Advanced Security Implementation.* Security Certified Program.

www.ingramcontent.com/pod-product-compliance
Ingram Content Group UK Ltd.
Pitfield, Milton Keynes, MK11 3LW, UK
UKHW041433180426
11947UKWH00007B/420